JAN – 6 2020

TURKEYS

Julie Murray

Big Buddy Books

An Imprint of Abdo Publishing
abdobooks.com

abdobooks.com

Published by Abdo Publishing, a division of ABDO, PO Box 398166, Minneapolis, Minnesota 55439.
Copyright © 2020 by Abdo Consulting Group, Inc. International copyrights reserved in all countries.
No part of this book may be reproduced in any form without written permission from the publisher.
Big Buddy Books™ is a trademark and logo of Abdo Publishing.

Printed in the United States of America, North Mankato, Minnesota
052019
092019

THIS BOOK CONTAINS
RECYCLED MATERIALS

Design: Sarah DeYoung, Mighty Media, Inc.
Production: Mighty Media, Inc.
Editor: Liz Salzmann
Cover Photograph: Shutterstock
Interior Photographs: iStockphoto (p. 21); Shutterstock (pp. 4–5, 6, 9, 10, 13, 15, 16, 17, 19, 23, 25, 27, 28–29)

Library of Congress Control Number: 2018939896

Publisher's Cataloging-in-Publication Data
Names: Murray, Julie, author.
Title: Turkeys / by Julie Murray.
Description: Minneapolis, Minnesota : Abdo Publishing, 2020. | Series:
       Animal kingdom | Includes online resources and index.
Identifiers: ISBN 9781532116568 (lib.bdg.) | ISBN 9781532158056 (ebook)
Subjects: LCSH: Turkeys--Juvenile literature. | Birds--Juvenile literature. |
       Birds--Behavior--Juvenile literature.
Classification: DDC 598.645--dc23

Contents

Turkeys 4

What They Look Like 8

Where They Live................................14

Eating 18

A Turkey's Life 22

Poults 26

Glossary..30

Online Resources................................31

Index 32

TURKEYS

Turkeys have lived in North America for thousands of years. American settlers hunted turkeys. **Native Americans** were the first people to raise turkeys for food.

Turkey is a favorite food for many people today. Some people hunt wild turkeys and eat them. People can buy turkey meat at stores too.

Wild turkeys are found throughout most of the United States.

5

Chickens are the most common poultry.

Turkeys are **poultry**. Poultry are birds that people raise for food. Other poultry are chickens, ducks, and geese.

WHAT THEY LOOK LIKE

>>>>>>>

Farm turkeys may have white, black, brown, red, or green feathers. Most wild turkeys have reddish-brown or gray feathers. Turkeys have no feathers on their necks and heads.

Male turkeys look different from female turkeys. Males are bigger and have ruffled, more colorful feathers.

SNOOD

WATTLE

A turkey's wattle and
snood are commonly red.

Turkeys have **wattles** that hang at their throats. They have **snoods** that hang above their beaks. Male turkeys, or toms, have **spurs** on their legs.

Farm turkeys are heavier than wild turkeys. Many farm turkeys are too heavy to fly. Farm toms can weigh up to 40 pounds (18 kg). Female turkeys, or hens, are smaller and lighter.

Wild turkeys can fly and move faster than farm turkeys. Wild toms weigh between 10 and 16 pounds (5 and 7 kg).

Wild turkeys can run 25 miles an hour (40 kmh) for short periods of time.

WHERE THEY LIVE

Farm turkeys live in many places around the world. Wild turkeys live in the United States, Mexico, and Guatemala.

The colorful ocellated turkey lives in Mexico and Guatemala.

Wild turkeys live for three to four years.

16

Wild turkeys live in forests, fields, and near croplands. At night, wild turkeys fly into the trees to roost.

Roosting in trees helps keep turkeys safe from predators.

EATING

Farm turkeys eat wheat, corn, and seeds. They also eat **insects** they find on the ground. Farmers give their turkeys clean water every day.

Farmers give turkeys special food to help them grow.

19

Wild turkeys spend much of their time searching for food. They often **scratch** the ground while searching. Wild turkeys eat **insects**, **acorns**, berries, and nuts.

Wild turkeys spend their days looking for food.

21

A TURKEY'S LIFE

Farmers take care of their turkeys. Some farmers let their turkeys run around outside. They stay inside a **shed** at night.

Free-range turkeys get to walk around outside at farms.

Some wild turkeys live together in flocks. Flocks look for food together. Some flocks only have toms. Other flocks only have hens and their young. Some turkey flocks have toms and hens.

Why Turkeys "Gobble"

Toms look for **mates** in late winter and early spring. They do special things to get the hens' attention. Toms puff out their body feathers and make "gobble" sounds. Toms will spread their tail feathers too.

POULTS

Hens lay between 10 and 15 eggs. A mother hen sits on her eggs to keep them warm. This is called **incubation**. Incubation helps the babies grow inside the eggs. They will **hatch** after about four weeks.

Mother hens rarely leave their eggs. A mother hen moves just once an hour to turn the eggs.

Male and female poults look the same until they are about 14 weeks old.

Baby turkeys are called **poults**. A poult has a special egg tooth. The poult uses its egg tooth to break out of the egg. Newly **hatched** poults have soft **down** feathers. They can walk and eat right away.

After about two weeks, poults grow adult feathers. Poults that live on farms stay **indoors**. Farmers may let them go outside when they are six weeks old.

Glossary

acorn—the seed from an oak tree.

down—soft, fluffy feathers.

hatch—to be born from an egg.

incubation—keeping eggs warm until they hatch.

indoors—inside a building.

insect—a small animal that has six legs and three main parts to its body.

mate—a partner to join with in order to reproduce, or have babies.

Native Americans—the very first people who lived in America.

poult—a young turkey.

poultry—birds that farmers raise for food.

scratch—to rub or scrape with a beak, claws, or fingernails.

shed—a small simple building.

snood—loose skin that hangs above a turkey's beak.

spur—a sharp, pointed part.

wattle—the flap of skin that hangs at a turkey's throat.

Online Resources

Booklinks
NONFICTION NETWORK
FREE! ONLINE NONFICTION RESOURCES

To learn more about turkeys, please visit **abdobooklinks.com** or scan this QR code. These links are routinely monitored and updated to provide the most current information available.

Index

acorns **20**

American settlers **4**

berries **20**

chickens **6, 7**

corn **18**

ducks **7**

egg tooth **29**

eggs **26, 27, 29**

farm turkeys **8, 12, 14, 18, 19, 22, 23, 29**

feathers **8, 9, 25, 29**

flocks **24**

geese **7**

Guatemala **14, 15**

hens **9, 12, 24, 25, 26, 27**

incubation **26**

insects **18, 20**

Mexico **14, 15**

Native Americans **4**

North America **4**

nuts **20**

ocellated turkeys **15**

poultry **6, 7**

poults **26, 28, 29**

predators **17**

roosting **17**

seeds **18**

snoods **10, 11**

spurs **11**

toms **9, 11, 12, 24, 25**

United States **5, 14**

wattles **10, 11**

wheat **18**

wild turkeys **4, 5, 8, 12, 13, 14, 16, 17, 20, 21, 24**